BIOGRAPHIES

GEORGE WASHINGTON

by Laura K. Murray

PEBBLE
a capstone imprint

Pebble Explore is published by Pebble, an imprint of Capstone.
1710 Roe Crest Drive
North Mankato, Minnesota 56003
www.capstonepub.com

Library of Congress Cataloging-in-Publication data is available on the Library of Congress website.
ISBN: 978-1-9771-1359-7 (library binding)
ISBN: 978-1-9771-1803-5 (paperback)
ISBN: 978-1-9771-1367-2 (eBook PDF)

Summary: Explores the life, challenges, and accomplishments of George Washington, the very first president of the United States.

Image Credits
Alamy: Lebrecht Music & Arts, 20; Library of Congress: 10, 12, 13, 26; National Gallery of Art: Andrew W. Mellon Collection, cover, 1, 29, Gift of Thomas Jefferson Coolidge IV in memory of his great-grandfather, Thomas Jefferson Coolidge, his grandfather, Thomas Jefferson Coolidge II, and his father, Thomas Jefferson Coolidge III, 27; Newscom: akg-images, 7, Everett Collection, 8, Picture History, 19; North Wind Picture Archives: 14, 15, 21; Shutterstock: critterbiz, 25, Olena Rodina (geometric background), cover, back cover, 2, 29, Victorian Traditions, 5; The Metropolitan Museum of Art: Bequest of William Nelson, 1905, 23, Gift of John Stewart Kennedy, 1897, 17

Editorial Credits
Christopher Harbo, editor; Elyse White, designer; Jo Miller and Svetlana Zhurkin, media researchers; Katy LaVigne, production specialist

All internet sites appearing in back matter were available and accurate when this book was sent to press.

Printed and bound in China.
2489

Table of Contents

Words in **bold** are in the glossary.

Who Was George Washington?

George Washington is called The Father of His Country. He led the army that won the **Revolutionary War** (1775–1783). This war helped the United States become its own country. Then he became the first **president** of the United States.

George was a brave and truthful leader. He believed the country was strongest when people worked together. He helped make the United States of America what it is today.

Growing Up George

George was born nearly 300 years ago on February 22, 1732. His family lived on a large farm in Virginia. Virginia was one of 13 **colonies** in North America. It was owned by Great Britain.

George grew up in a big family. He had six brothers and three sisters. His family owned many farms in Virginia. They had **enslaved** people to do the work on the farms. George grew up on Ferry Farm.

George

When George was 11, his father died. George had to help his mother and siblings run the family's farms. He also learned subjects at home until age 15. He learned math and writing. He read about good manners and being truthful.

George liked to explore. At age 16, he took a trip with men who measured and mapped land. The maps showed what the land looked like. George learned a lot. The next year, he got his first job doing the same thing.

George

George joined the Virginia army at age 20. He led his soldiers during the French and Indian War (1754–1763). This war was fought between British and French colonies. George and the Virginian army fought for the British. Both the British and the French had American Indians fighting for them.

George learned a lot during the French and Indian War. He became a better leader. He learned how to make good plans for battles and wars.

Family and Hobbies

George married Martha Custis in 1759 at age 26. Martha had two children from her first marriage. George acted as a father to them.

George and Martha's wedding

The Washingtons lived at Mount Vernon. It was one of the Washington family farms. But Martha often worked by George's side. When he went to war, she stayed in the army camps. She raised money for the soldiers. She also helped them as a nurse.

George enjoyed many hobbies. He liked fishing and hunting. He also liked to swim and wrestle. George was a good dancer and horse rider.

George liked farming. Different crops were planted on his farms. They grew corn, wheat, potatoes, and turnips. A lot of this work was done by enslaved people. George also made the house at Mount Vernon bigger.

Leading a New Country

After the French and Indian War, George began working with the leaders of the colonies. They felt that Great Britain was ruling them unfairly. They wanted to be free to make their own country.

The Revolutionary War started in 1775. The colonies fought for **freedom** from Great Britain. They picked George to lead their army.

George and his army crossed the Delaware River.

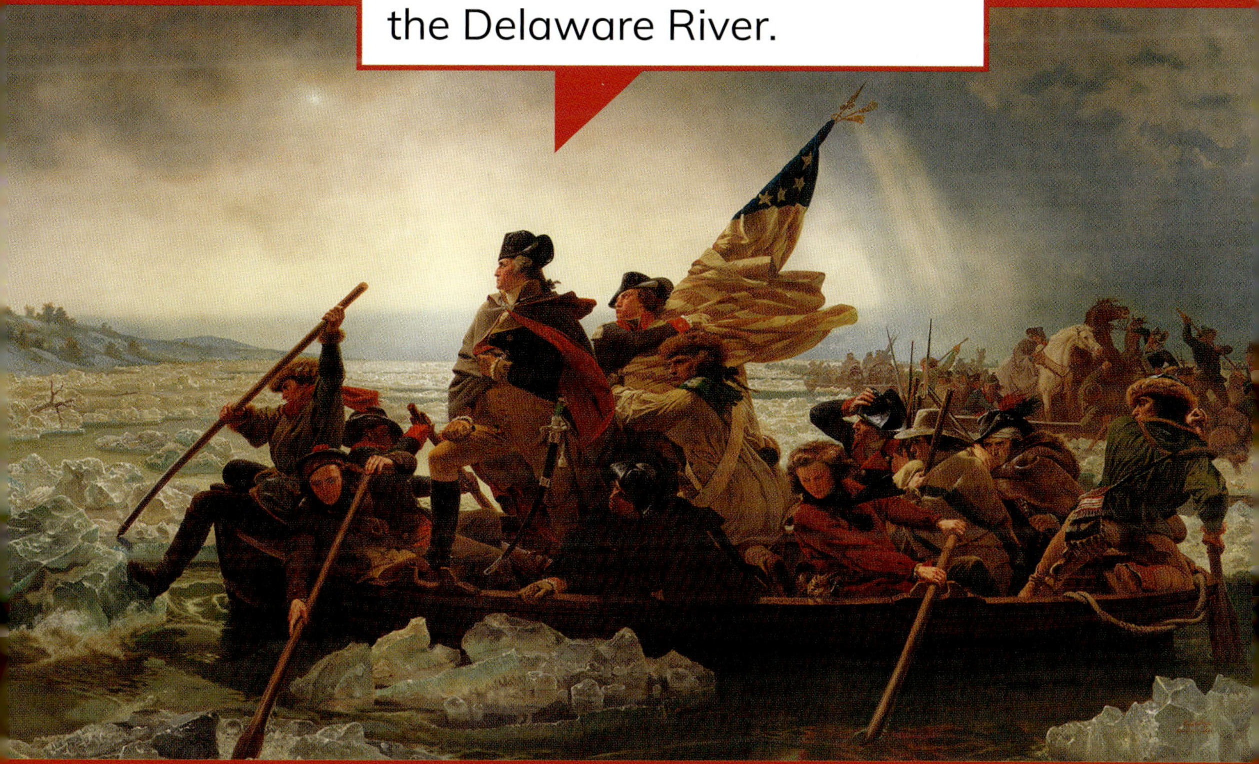

The next year, on Christmas Day, George led his men across the Delaware River. They took the enemy by surprise. It was George's first big win of the war.

In 1783, the colonies won the war. Afterward, George wanted to return to his farm. But the new country needed help forming a **government**.

In 1787, leaders from the colonies met to talk about a new government. George led the meeting. The meeting's members wrote the **U.S. Constitution**. It showed how the U.S. government would work.

George led the meeting to write the U.S. Constitution.

The new country also needed a president. George won all of the **votes**! He became the first U.S. president on April 30, 1789.

George as president in 1793

George worked hard as president. He helped Benjamin Franklin, Thomas Jefferson, and other leaders set up a new government. Many people did not agree on how the new country should be run.

In 1792, George was **elected** president again. Many people even wanted him to be president a third time. But George wanted to go home. In 1796, he wrote a letter to say goodbye. In it he said that Americans should work together as one country.

Back to Mount Vernon

George and Martha moved back to Mount Vernon. George worked on his land and house. But he still wanted to help his country. In 1798, George was made the leader of the U.S. Army.

George died on December 14, 1799. He was 67 years old. He was buried at Mount Vernon. People were sad that their first president had died. People in many cities came together to honor him. Some people in other countries did too.

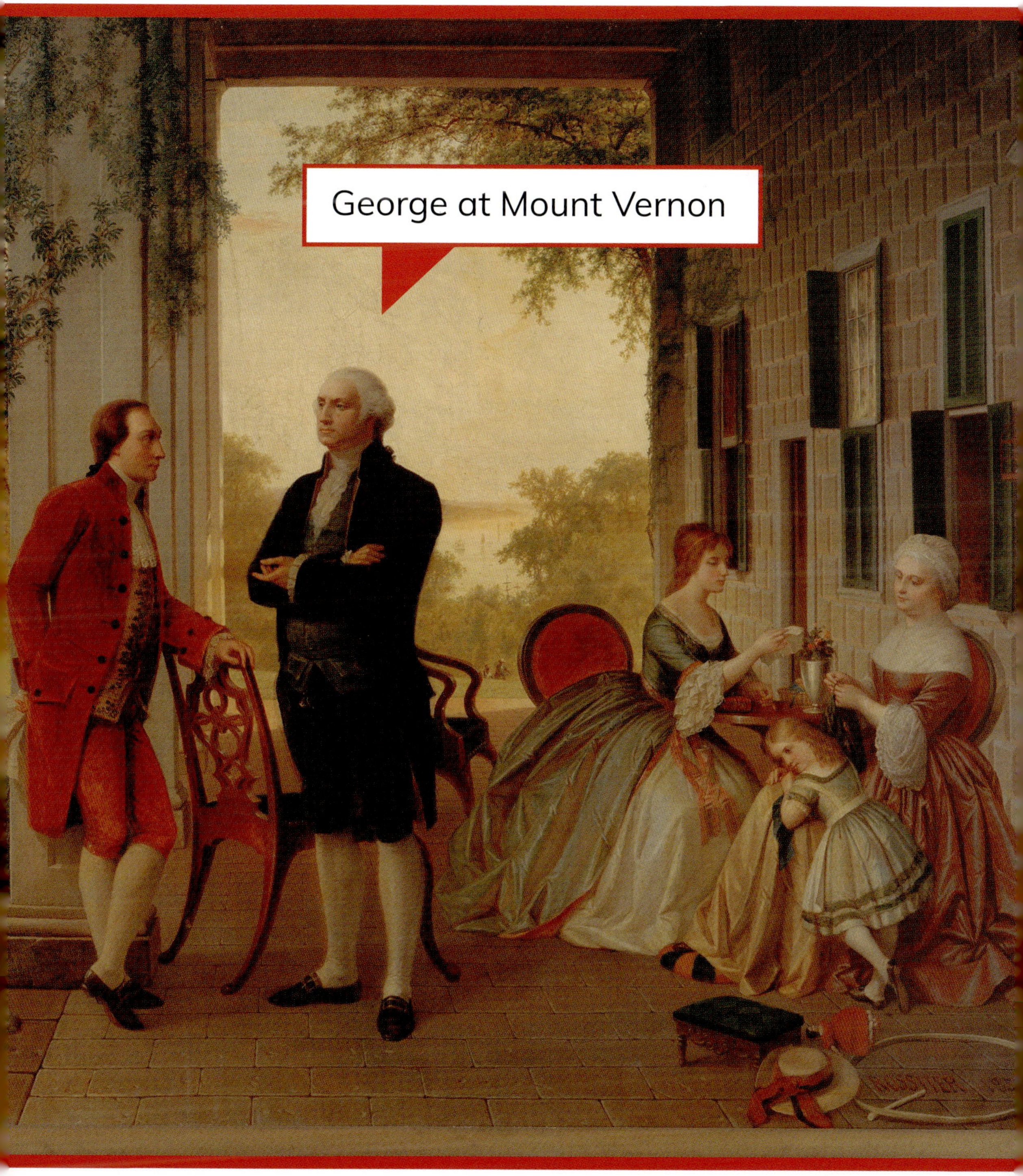
George at Mount Vernon

Remembering Washington

People remember George Washington in many ways. He is on the quarter and $1 bill. George's face is on Mount Rushmore in South Dakota. Americans also remember George's birthday on the third Monday of February. This holiday is called Presidents' Day.

Many places are named after George too. Washington, D.C., is the U.S. **capital**. The state of Washington is also named after him.

George
Mount Rushmore

Many people remember George with stories. One story says he chopped down a cherry tree as a boy. Then he told his father about what he had done. The story is made up, but it shows how important the truth was to George.

George Washington was a great leader. He believed in working together. He helped when the United States needed him. He will always be known as The Father of His Country.

Important Dates

February 22, 1732	George Washington is born in Virginia.
1738	George's family moves to Ferry Farm in Virginia.
1752	George joins the Virginia army.
January 6, 1759	George marries Martha Custis.
1775	George is picked to lead the army for the colonies during the Revolutionary War.
1787	George is picked to lead the meeting to write the U.S. Constitution.
April 30, 1789	George becomes the first president of the United States.
1792	George is elected U.S. president for a second time.
1796	George leaves office and returns with Martha to Mount Vernon.
1798	George is made the leader of the U.S. Army.
December 14, 1799	George Washington dies at home at Mount Vernon in Virginia at the age of 67.

Fast Facts

Name:
George Washington

Role:
First president of the United States, often called The Father of His Country

Life dates:
February 22, 1732 to December 14, 1799

Key accomplishments:
George Washington led the army for the colonies during the Revolutionary War. He also led the meeting to write the U.S. Constitution. In 1789, George became the very first president of the United States.

Glossary

capital (KA-puh-tuhl)—the city in a country where the government is based

colony (KAH-luh-nee)—an area that has been settled by people from another country and is owned by that country

elect (i-LEKT)—to choose a leader by voting

enslave (en-SLAYV)—to make someone lose their freedom

freedom (FREE-duhm)—being able to live the way you want

government (GUHV-urn-muhnt)—the group of people who make rules and decisions for a country or state

president (PREZ-uh-duhnt)—the highest elected job in a class, business, or country

Revolutionary War (rev-uh-LOO-shuhn-air-ee WOR)—the American colonies' fight from 1775 to 1783 for freedom from Great Britain

U.S. Constitution (YOO ESS kahn-stuh-TOO-shuhn)—the plan for how the U.S. government works

vote (VOHT)—a choice made in an election

Read More

Albee, Sarah. George *Washington: The First President*. New York: Harper, 2017.

Bednarchuck, Bruce. *Our First President: George Washington*. Minneapolis: Cantata Learning, 2015.

Kirkman, Marissa. *The Life and Times of George Washington and the American Revolution*. North Mankato, MN: Capstone, 2017.

Internet Sites

Biography of President George Washington
https://www.ducksters.com/biography/uspresidents/georgewashington.php

George Washington: A National Treasure
https://www.georgewashington.si.edu/kids/non-flash.html

George Washington's Mount Vernon
https://www.mountvernon.org/george-washington

Index